Learn Number Skills

Colour each picture as you finish each page.

Written by Wendy and David Clemson
Illustrated by Roma Bishop

Ladybird

Maths talk

More

Look at the pictures of the toys.
Can you find the ducks and the balls?

Are there **more** ducks or **more** balls? ✓ the boxes.

Tick the correct box. ☐ 🦆   ☐ ⚽

Look at the pictures of the toys and count them again.
Are there **more** ducks or **more** crowns?

☐ 🦆   ☐ 👑

more balls or balloons?   **more** frogs or stickers?

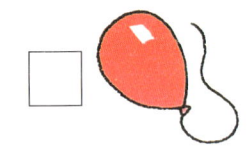

☐ ⚽   ☐ 🎈   ☐ 🐸   ☐ 🐸

Less or fewer

Less or fewer means the opposite of more.
Count the toys in the picture again.

Are there **fewer** whistles or **fewer** dinosaurs?

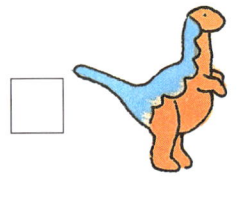

☐ 🔔   ☐ 🦖

Are there **fewer** ghost erasers or **fewer** pencils?

☐ 👻   ☐ ✏️

Same

Count the toys in the party bags.
How many toys are in each bag?
Tick the bags that have the **same**
number of toys in them.

Here are some more toys. Count them.
Draw lines to match the toys to the correct numbers.

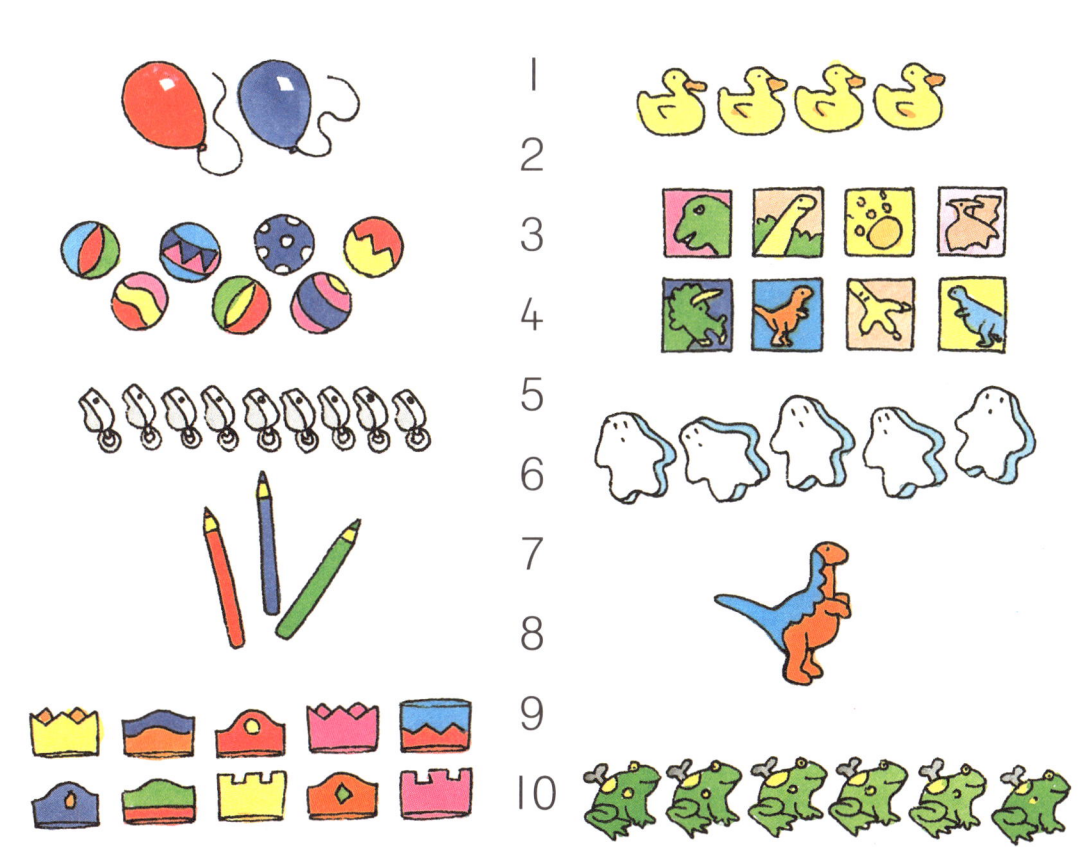

1
2
3
4
5
6
7
8
9
10

Parent point: 'More', 'less', and 'the same' are mathematical comparisons we make in everyday life. Use the pictures of the toys on page 2 to familiarise your child with counting and comparing. Collect together some toys. Your child can use these for grouping and counting practice.

Addition to 5

Adding is putting together to make a **total**.

1 and  2 makes  3 altogether

Put together the number of spiders in each box.
Draw and write the answer.

☐ and ☐ makes ☐ altogether

Now try these.

☐ and ☐ makes ☐ altogether

☐ and ☐ makes ☐ altogether

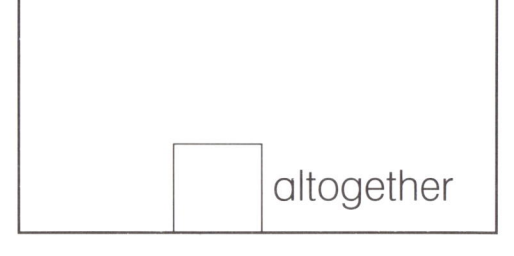

☐ and ☐ makes ☐ altogether

When we write additions we can use this sign **+**.
This means **and** or **add**.

We can use **=** as the sign for **makes** or **equals**.

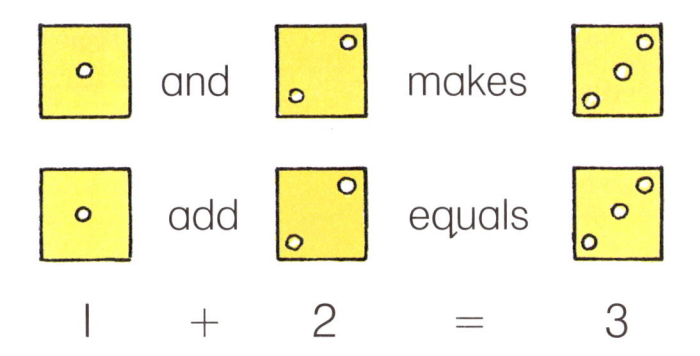

and   makes

add   equals

1   +   2   =   3

Remember **+** means **and** or **add**,
= means **makes** or **equals**.

Put in the signs to make additions. Say what they mean.

| 2   3   5 | | 1   3   4 |

Write in the numbers to show how many altogether.

1 + 2 = ☐   1 + 3 = ☐

2 + 3 = ☐   2 + 1 = ☐

3 + 1 = ☐   3 + 2 = ☐

2 + 2 = ☐   1 + 4 = ☐

Parent point: Give addition a context by using real objects. Collect together food tins or forks and spoons. Ask your child how many items there are altogether. Ask him or her to put items into groups, add the items up and call out the total. Or collect magazine pictures and use them in the same way.

Addition to 10

You have shown that you can add to 5. Well done!
Let's go up to 10 now.

See if you can add these. Draw and write the answers.

and makes altogether

and makes altogether

and makes altogether

and makes altogether

and makes altogether

and makes altogether

Remember we can use **+** for **and** or **add**,
= means **makes** or **equals**.

 🍎🍎🍎🍎🍎	and	 🍎	makes	 🍎🍎🍎🍎🍎🍎
5	add	1	equals	6
5	+	1	=	6

What are the answers to these additions?

2 + 5 = ☐   3 + 3 = ☐   9 + 1 = ☐

3 + 5 = ☐   4 + 2 = ☐   2 + 6 = ☐

4 + 6 = ☐   4 + 4 = ☐   2 + 8 = ☐

7 + 1 = ☐   8 + 1 = ☐   3 + 6 = ☐

6 + 2 = ☐   1 + 9 = ☐   4 + 5 = ☐

5 + 3 = ☐   3 + 4 = ☐   5 + 2 = ☐

Draw a line to join each addition to its answer.

6 + 3   5 + 1   9   8

1 + 7   5 + 5   10   6

Parent point: Encourage your child to move on to higher numbers once he or she is confident in adding to 5 successfully. You can help by using lots of real things for addition – biscuits, spoons or books, for example.

Subtraction to 5

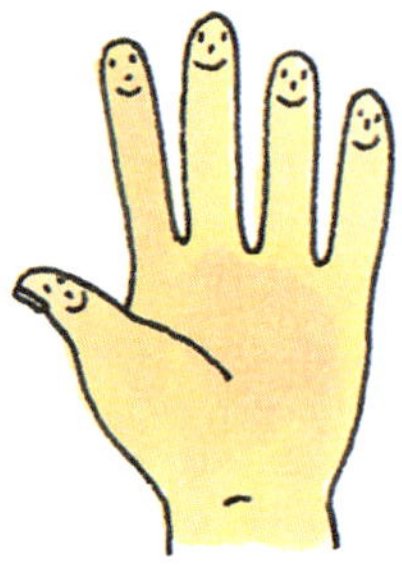

Hold up your hand.
Draw a little face on each of your fingers.
Make the faces hide.

When you hide or **take away** some faces, how many are left?

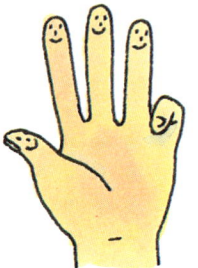

take away 1    take away 2    take away 3 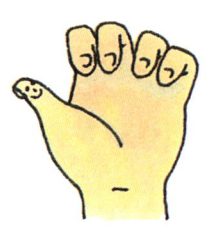   take away 4

When we write subtractions we can use this sign **−**.
It means **take away** or **subtract**.
We can use **=** as the sign for **leaves** or **equals**.

Here is an example of how we can use **subtraction**.

3 children, Lin, Rik and Sue, go to the library together to choose some books.

Rik goes home early. How many children does he leave at the library? ☐

We can write this as   3 take away 1 leaves 2
3 subtract 1 equals 2
3 − 1 = 2

Try these subtractions. Use your finger-faces to help you.
Draw and write the answers.

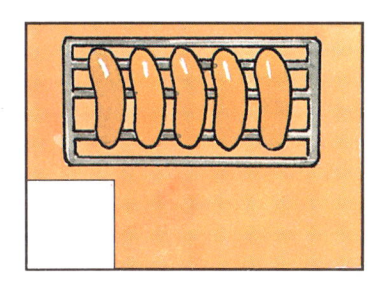

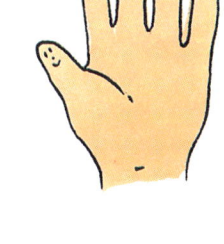

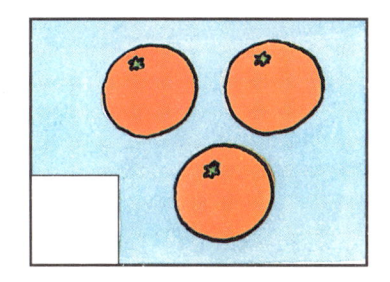

take away ☐ leaves ☐

take away ☐ leaves ☐

take away ☐ leaves ☐

Put in the − and the = signs to make subtractions.
Say what they mean.

| 3 | 1 | 2 |

| 4 | 2 | 2 |

Write in the numbers
that show how many
are left behind in
these subtractions.

4 − 1 = ☐   3 − 2 = ☐

5 − 2 = ☐   4 − 3 = ☐

Parent point: For children who are beginning to learn subtraction, taking away and leaving behind are the important ideas. Try playing with subtractions using pens, buttons and dried beans. Encourage the use of fingers to help calculate or count.

Subtraction to 10

Now that you are happy doing subtractions using numbers up to 5, why not try subtracting using numbers up to **10**?
Draw finger-faces on both your hands to help you.

Remember we can use − as the sign for
take away or **subtract**.
We can use = as the sign for **leaves** or **equals**.

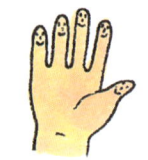

Look at the washing line. There are 9 shirts on it.

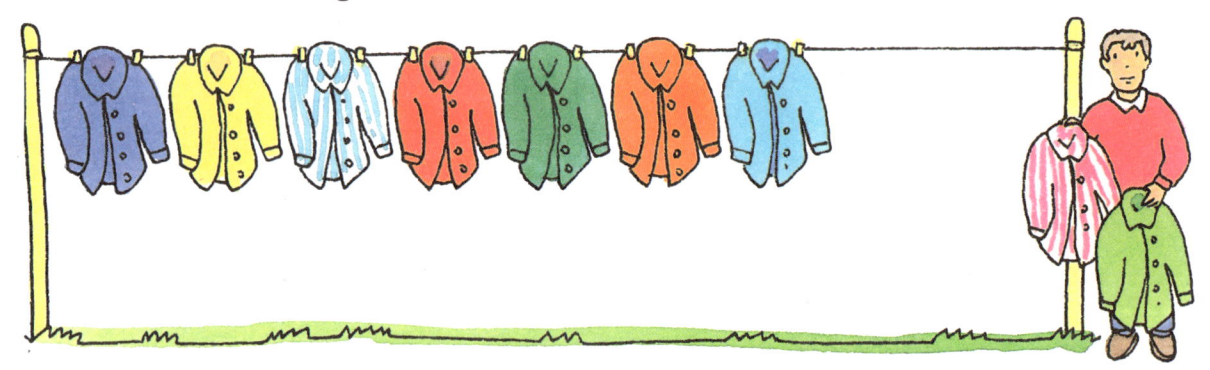

Look at the washing line now. Dad has taken 2 shirts away from the line.

How many are left behind?

We can write this as 9 take away 2 leaves 7
9 subtract 2 equals 7
9 − 2 = 7

10 ten

Try these subtractions. Draw and write your answers.

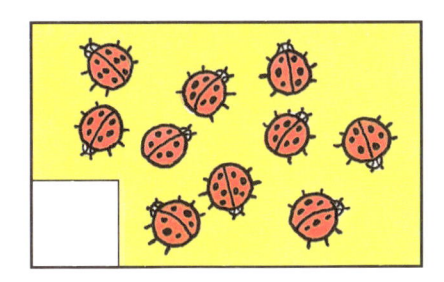

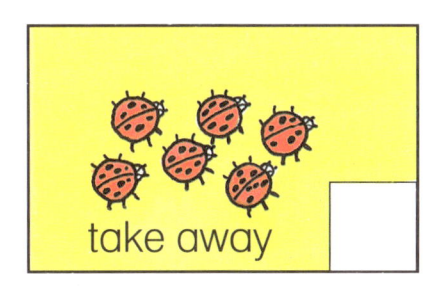

take away   leaves

take away   leaves

take away   leaves

Now try these subtractions. Use your finger faces to help.

8 – 4 =   8 – 2 =   9 – 4 =

9 – 1 =   6 – 2 =   7 – 3 =

7 – 1 =   9 – 5 =   7 – 6 =

6 – 5 =   7 – 2 =   6 – 3 =

8 – 7 =   8 – 3 =   9 – 2 =

7 – 4 =   6 – 4 =   8 – 6 =

Parent Point: Subtraction to 10 follows when your child can confidently subtract to 5. Demonstrate subtractions by allowing your child to group items, such as buttons, coins or pencils, and then take some of them away to leave some behind.

Number patterns and odds and evens

Here is some fruit.

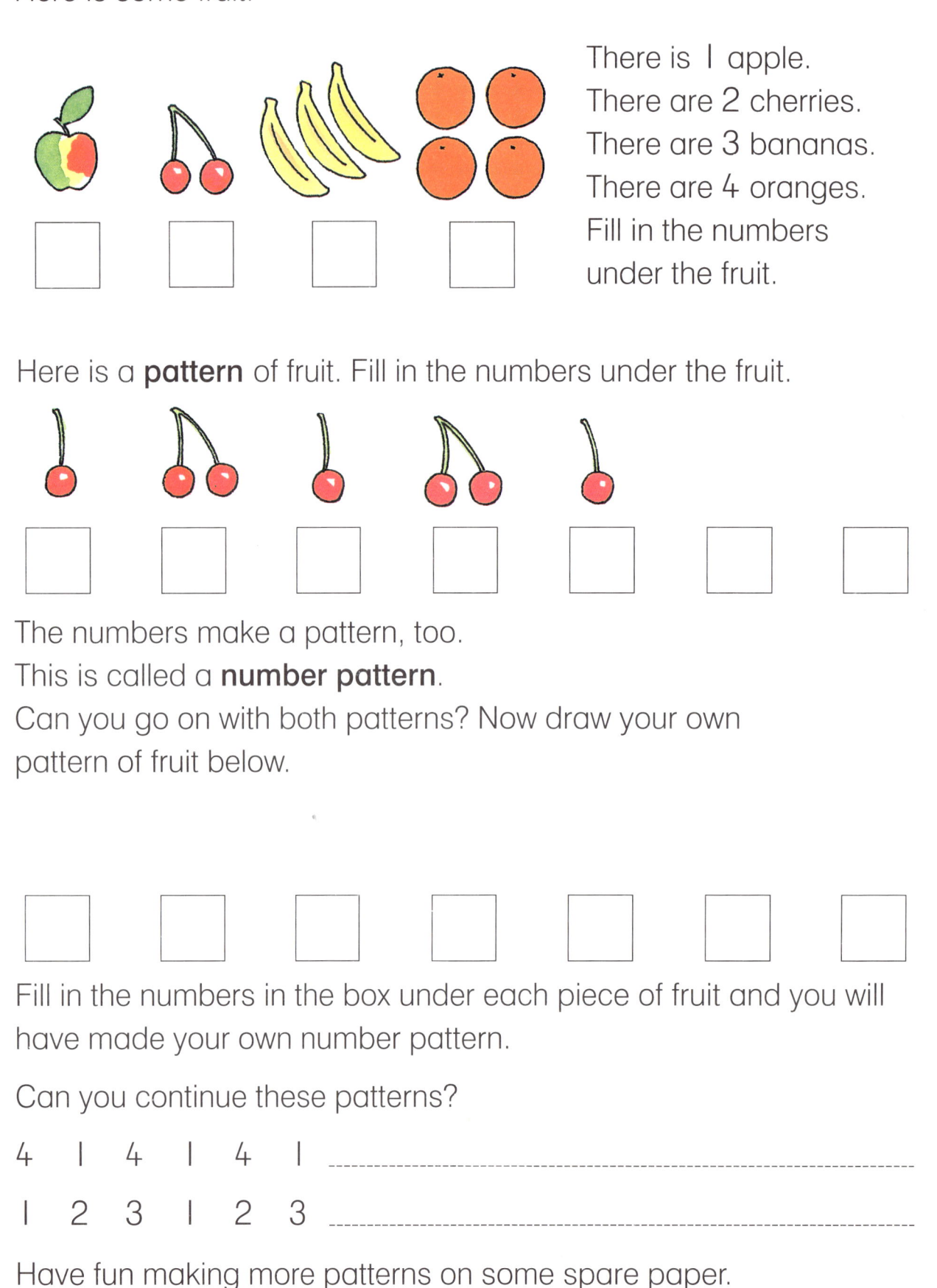

☐	☐	☐	☐

There is 1 apple.
There are 2 cherries.
There are 3 bananas.
There are 4 oranges.
Fill in the numbers under the fruit.

Here is a **pattern** of fruit. Fill in the numbers under the fruit.

☐ ☐ ☐ ☐ ☐ ☐ ☐

The numbers make a pattern, too.
This is called a **number pattern**.
Can you go on with both patterns? Now draw your own pattern of fruit below.

☐ ☐ ☐ ☐ ☐ ☐ ☐

Fill in the numbers in the box under each piece of fruit and you will have made your own number pattern.

Can you continue these patterns?

4 1 4 1 4 1 _____

1 2 3 1 2 3 _____

Have fun making more patterns on some spare paper.

Look at the numbers and colours on the chart.

The numbers coloured green are called **odd**.

The numbers coloured yellow are called **even**.

This shows that

1 is **odd**

2 is **even**

Look at the pattern again.

Write down all the **odd** numbers here.

| 1 | | | | | | | | 19 |

Write down all the **even** numbers here.

| 2 | | | | | | | | 20 |

The children have been to the fair.
They each have a lucky ticket.
Odd numbers win a toffee apple.
Even numbers win a fruit bar.
Draw a line to join each child to his or her prize.

| 1 |
| 2 |
| 3 |
| 4 |
| 5 |
| 6 |
| 7 |
| 8 |
| 9 |
| 10 |
| 11 |
| 12 |
| 13 |
| 14 |
| 15 |
| 16 |
| 17 |
| 18 |
| 19 |
| 20 |

Parent point: To help your child remember odd and even numbers, play 'noisy odds'. Ask your child to shout 'boo' when you say an odd number and 'shhshh' when you say an even number. Use counters to show how even numbers can always be split into two equal piles. This page is an introduction to *algebra*. Algebra means using symbols to show the relationships between numbers.

Finding patterns in addition and subtraction

Look carefully at the coloured beads below.
They are all together on a string. Can you find the patterns?
Say the additions next to each row of beads.

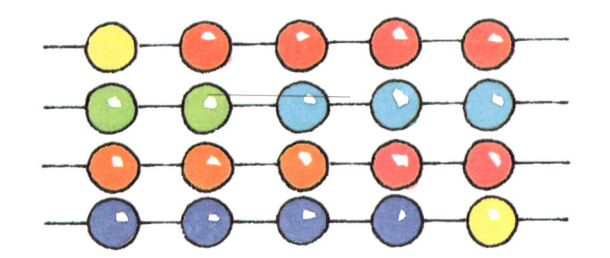

1 + 4
2 + 3
3 + 2
4 + 1

Have you noticed that 1 + 4 = 5
4 + 1 = 5

When you put 4 and 1 or 1 and 4 together,
they make 5.
Which other numbers can you put together
and make 5?

Here are some more ways of making 5. Say the additions next to each row.

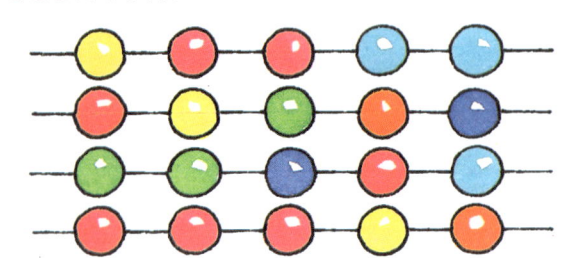

1 + 2 + 2
1 + 1 + 1 + 1 + 1
2 + 1 + 1 + 1
3 + 1 + 1

Write the additions that make these patterns of 6 next to each row.

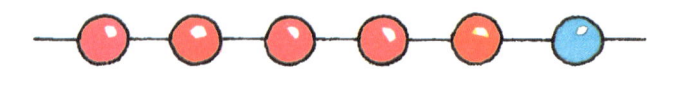

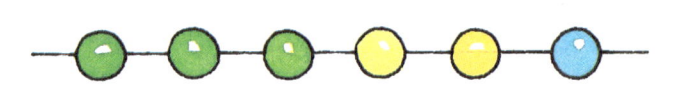

☐ + ☐

☐ + ☐ + ☐

☐ + ☐ + ☐

Now look at these beads. There are 10 beads in each row.
Some of the beads have been taken off the string,
leaving other beads behind.

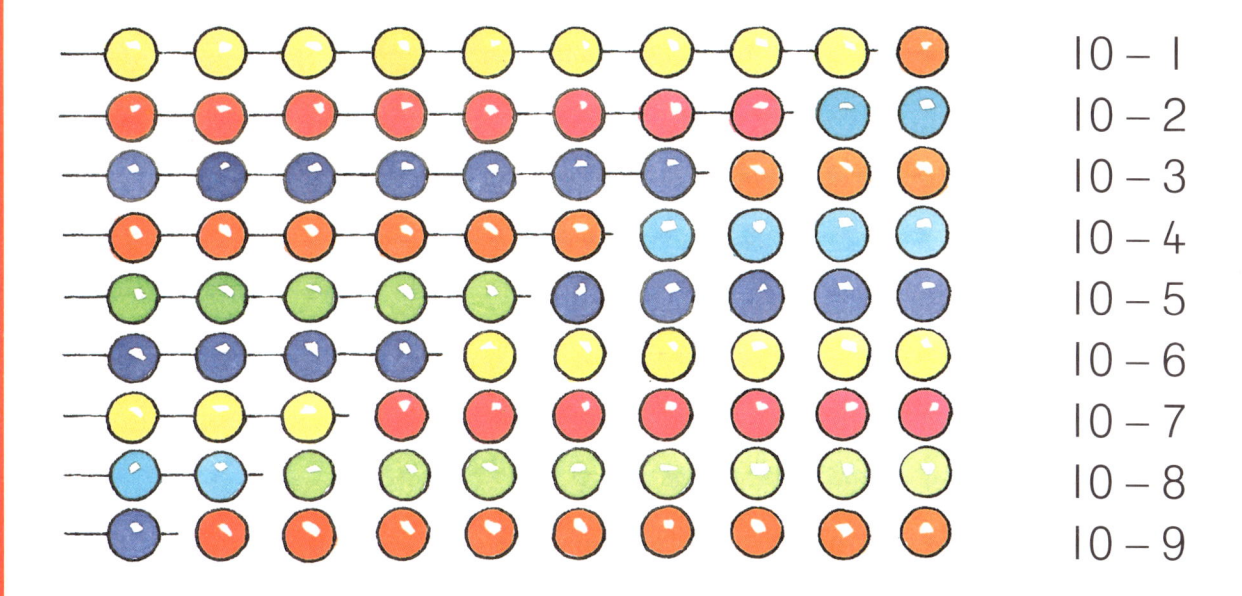

10 − 1
10 − 2
10 − 3
10 − 4
10 − 5
10 − 6
10 − 7
10 − 8
10 − 9

When you take 1 bead off the string, you leave 9 behind.
When you take 7 beads off the string, you leave 3 behind.

Here are some beads for you to colour.

Make your own number patterns with these.

Write the pattern you have coloured next to each row.

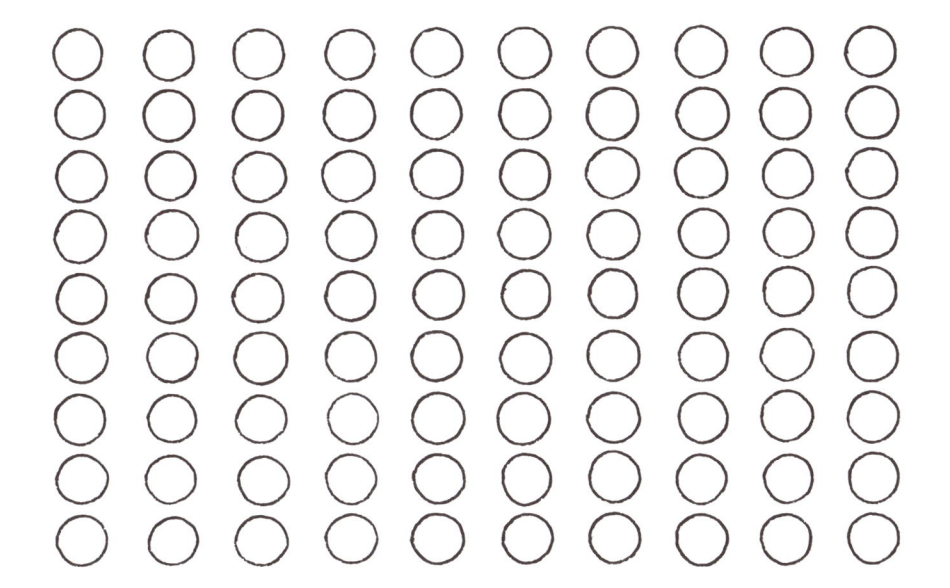

Parent point: Help your child to recognise number patterns which come in pairs, like 1 + 4 and 4 + 1, 2 + 3 and 3 + 2. These pairs always make the same total no matter which way round they come.

Missing numbers

The Number Detective looks for missing numbers.
He was given these additions and must find the missing numbers.

5 + 2 = ◯   5 + ◯ = 7   ◯ + 2 = 7

Now he has found the missing numbers.

5 + 2 = ⑦   5 + ② = 7   ⑤ + 2 = 7

Why not be a number detective too?
Find the missing numbers in these.

1 + ◯ = 2   2 + ◯ = 3   4 − ◯ = 3

These numbers are missing. Find where they go and write them in.

5   2   7   4

4 + ◯ = 6   ◯ + 5 = 10

1 + ◯ = 8   ◯ + 3 = 7

Play Match and Make

Cut out the cards above so that each card has one number on the back of it.

Match a number card to a picture card by laying picture cards and number cards alongside one another.

Play **Make Five** by setting out a row of picture cards that add up to five or a row of number cards that add up to five. Once you can do these easily, try mixing number and picture cards to make totals of five.

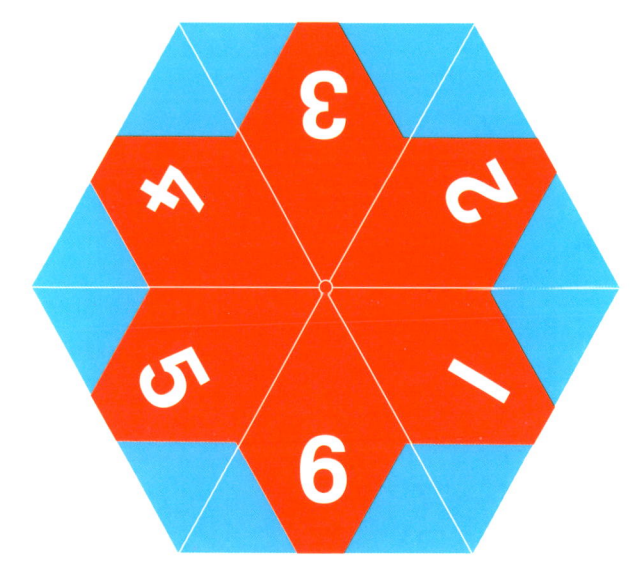

See overleaf for instructions to make spinner.

Cut out and use these ladybirds to help you count and calculate.

2	2	2	1	1	1
2	2	1	3	3	1
4	1	3	3	3	3
3	3	4	4	4	4
2	1	2	2	1	3

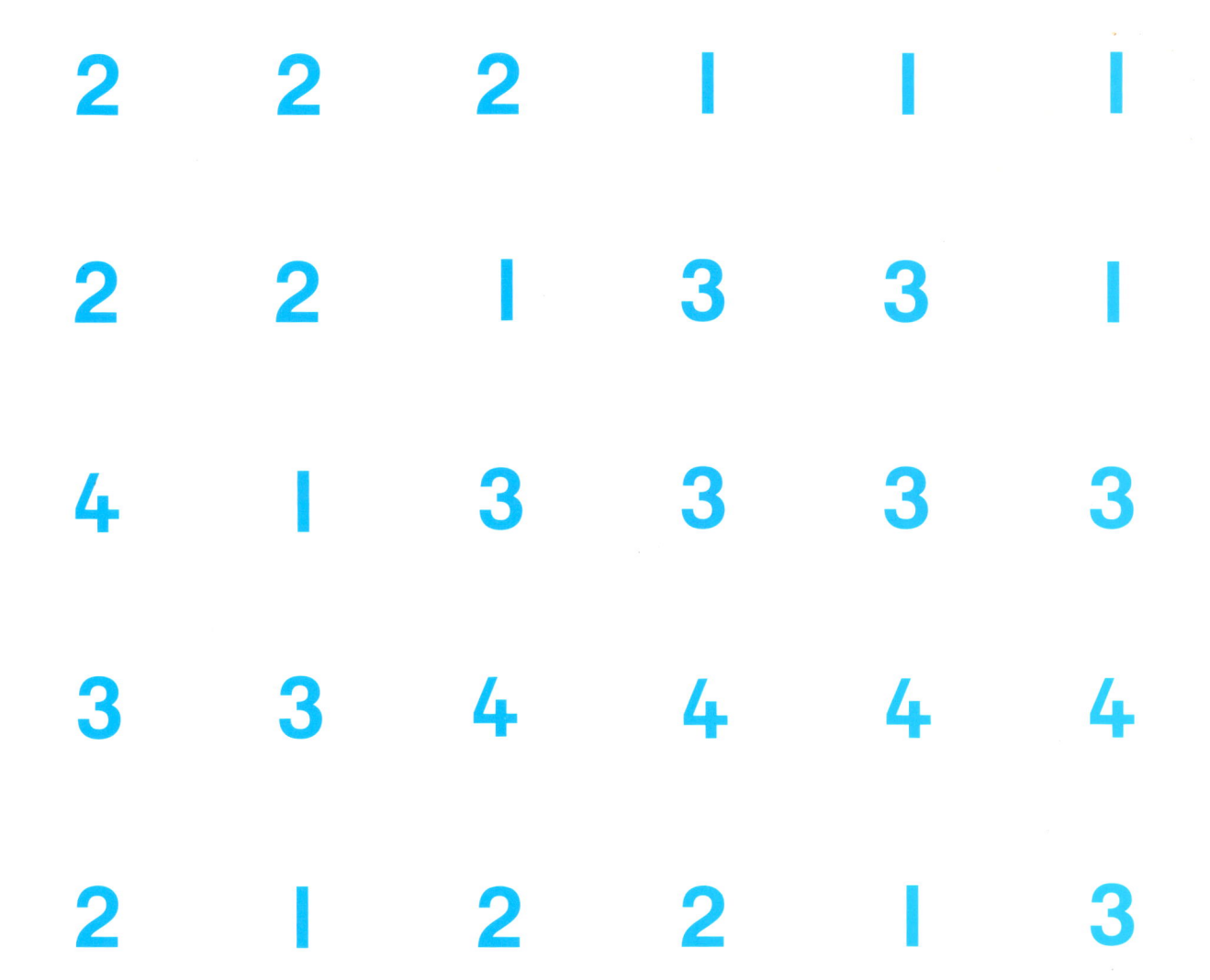

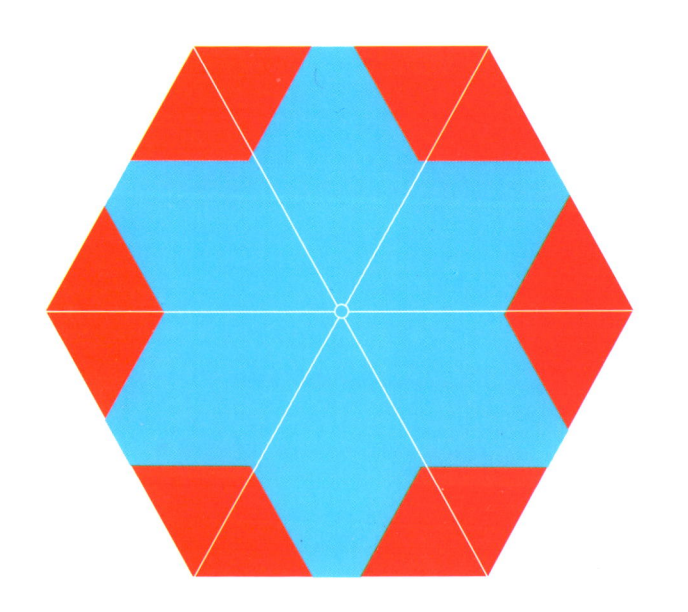

Cut out the spinner. Make a small hole in the centre. Push a used match into the hole. Use it for the **Star Challenge** game.

Where the spinner rests shows the number of spaces you can move.

7 + 2   4 + 4   3 + 6   5 + 1   2 + 2   4 + 2

9 − 6   7 − 2   2 − 1   5 − 4   8 − 5   4 − 3

5 + 3   1 + 6   5 + 5   6 − 3   3 − 1   7 − 5

Star Challenge

*To play **Star Challenge** you need:*

2–4 players

Playing board (overleaf)

Star cards (cut out from below)

Cardboard playing pieces, buttons or pasta shapes

Spinner (cut out from this insert)

Make sure you have read the instructions before you cut out the board and cards!

How to play:

Choose a playing piece each and put it at the start on the **playing board**. Shuffle star cards and place face down in a pile, next to playing board.

Take turns to spin the spinner and move the number of spaces the spinner shows.

Players who land on a **star space** pick up a star card and do the calculation. They then move that number of spaces (forward if addition, and backwards if subtraction).

If a player's move takes them backwards, past the start, they stay on the start square. They begin to play again when it is their next turn.

To finish, a player may go onto or beyond the last square (they do not need to land on the last square exactly). Good luck!

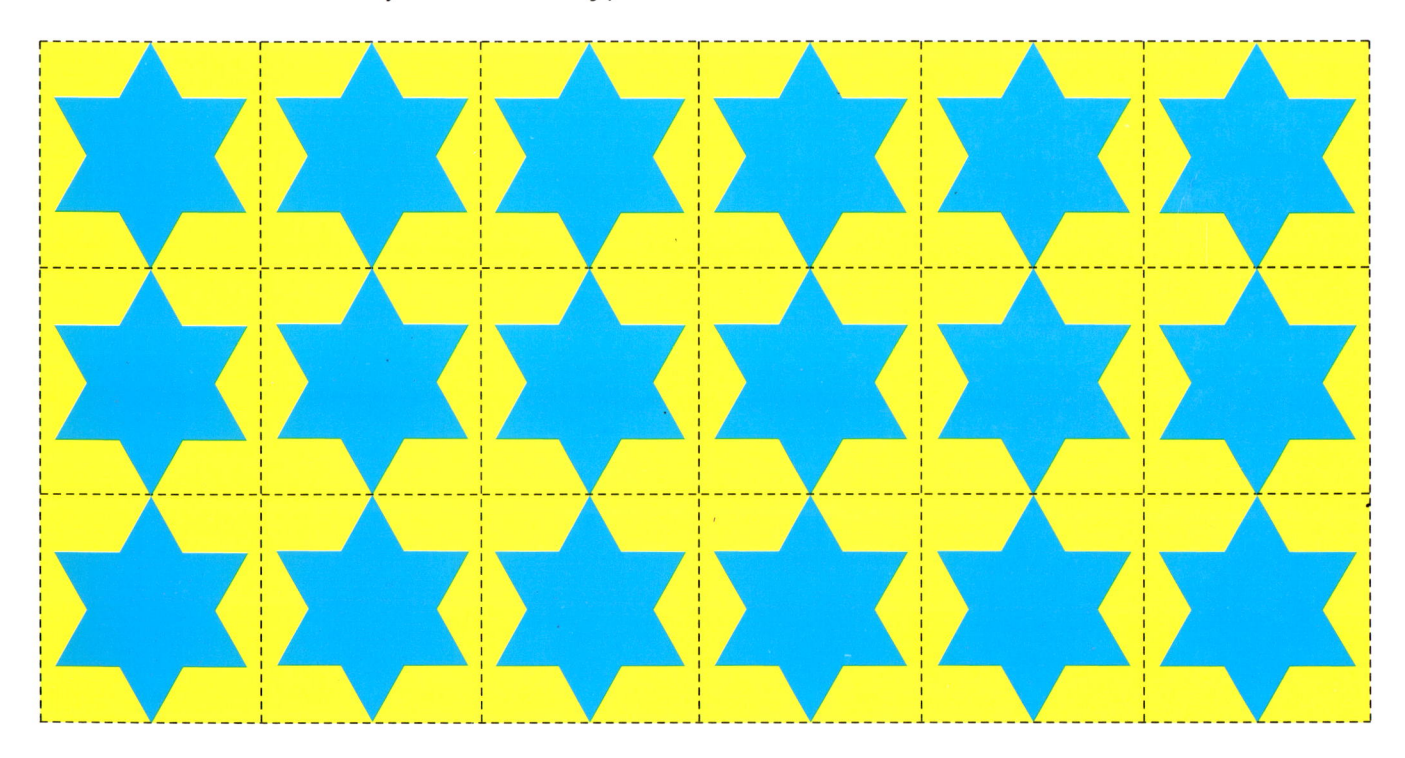

Which numbers are missing here?
Write them in.

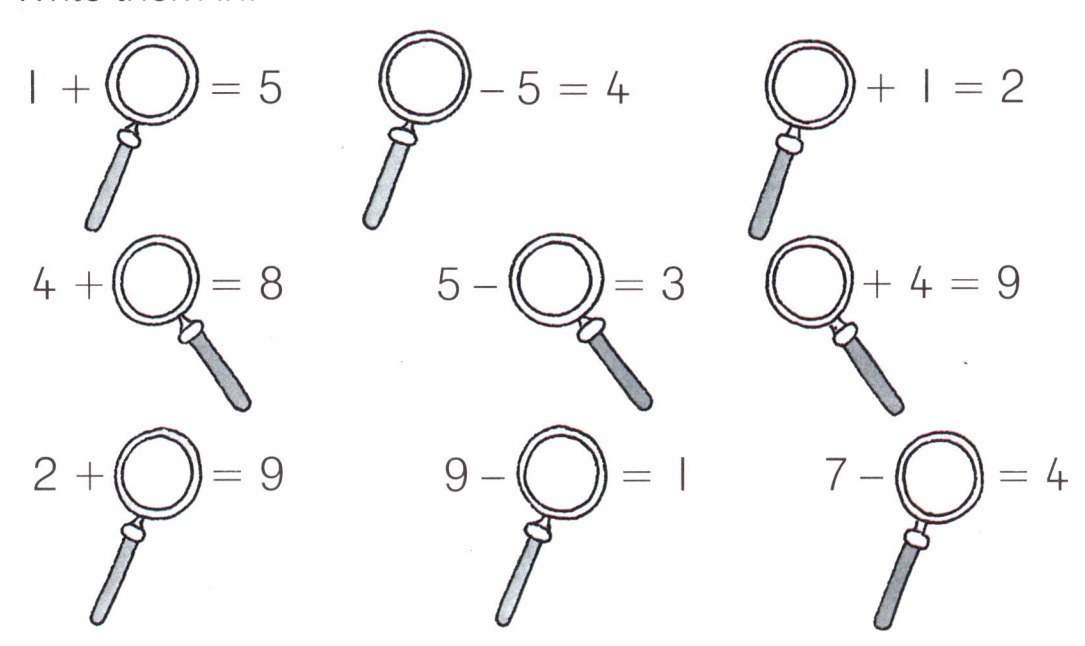

1 + ◯ = 5   ◯ − 5 = 4   ◯ + 1 = 2

4 + ◯ = 8   5 − ◯ = 3   ◯ + 4 = 9

2 + ◯ = 9   9 − ◯ = 1   7 − ◯ = 4

Play the detective and follow these trails to find the missing numbers.

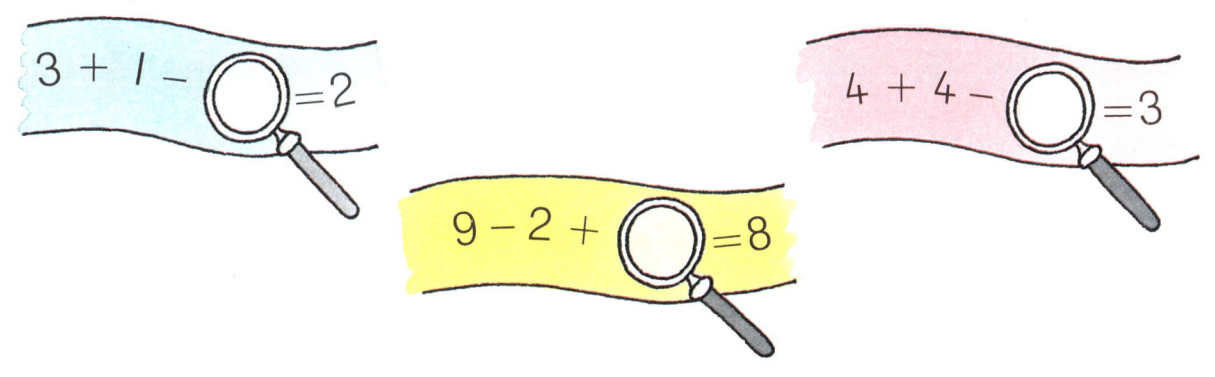

3 + 1 − ◯ = 2

4 + 4 − ◯ = 3

9 − 2 + ◯ = 8

Count the dots on the dice. What is the total?

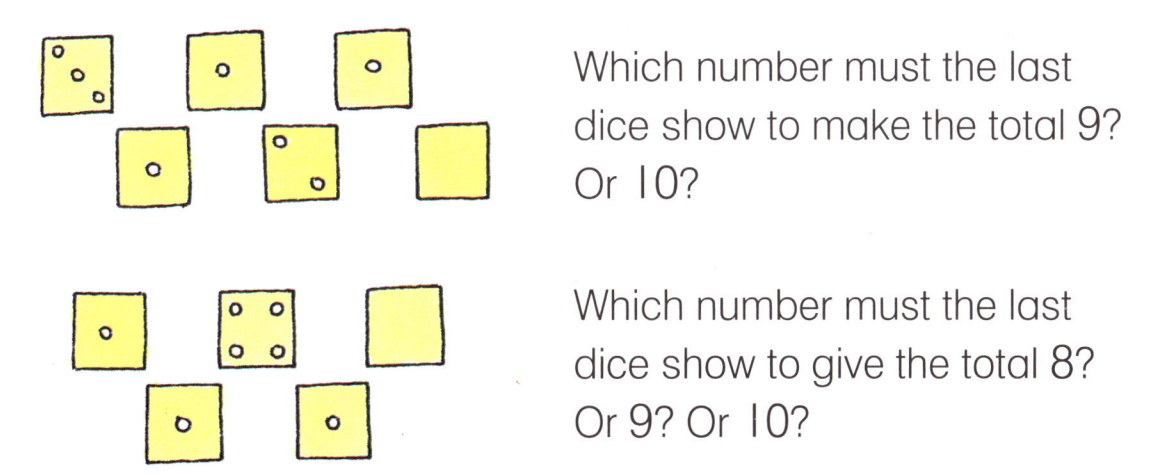

Which number must the last dice show to make the total 9? Or 10?

Which number must the last dice show to give the total 8? Or 9? Or 10?

Parent point: Finding missing numbers helps children notice how numbers combine to give common totals. Use a set of dominoes to make up puzzles. For example, lay out two or three dominoes. Ask your child to find a domino that, when added to the dominoes he or she can already see, will make a given total.

Place values – tens and units

Where we put or 'place' a digit in a number tells us its value.

Each bag only holds 10 marbles. There are two bags of ten marbles **and** four extra marbles.

Can you count how many marbles there are altogether? ☐

24 is the same as 10 + 10 + 4.
There are 2 lots of ten marbles and 4 marbles on their own.
We say that this is 2 **tens** and 4 **units**   2   4
                                                  tens units

Here are some more numbers set out as tens and units.

36	17	43
3　6	1　7	4　3
tens　units	tens　units	tens　units

Write how many tens and units are in these numbers.

17　　　　　　　36　　　　　　　54

ten　units　　tens　units　　tens　units

Write down these numbers.　　6 tens and 9 units is ☐

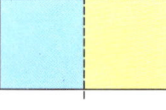

7 tens and 1 unit is ☐　　5 tens and 5 units is ☐

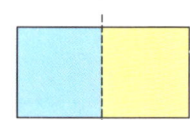

Can you think of some more numbers that have tens and units?

Colour the houses. Say which number each house has.
Can you write these numbers in tens and units?

[ ] tens [ ] units   [ ] tens [ ] unit   [ ] tens [ ] units

Draw a line to match each number to its tens and units.

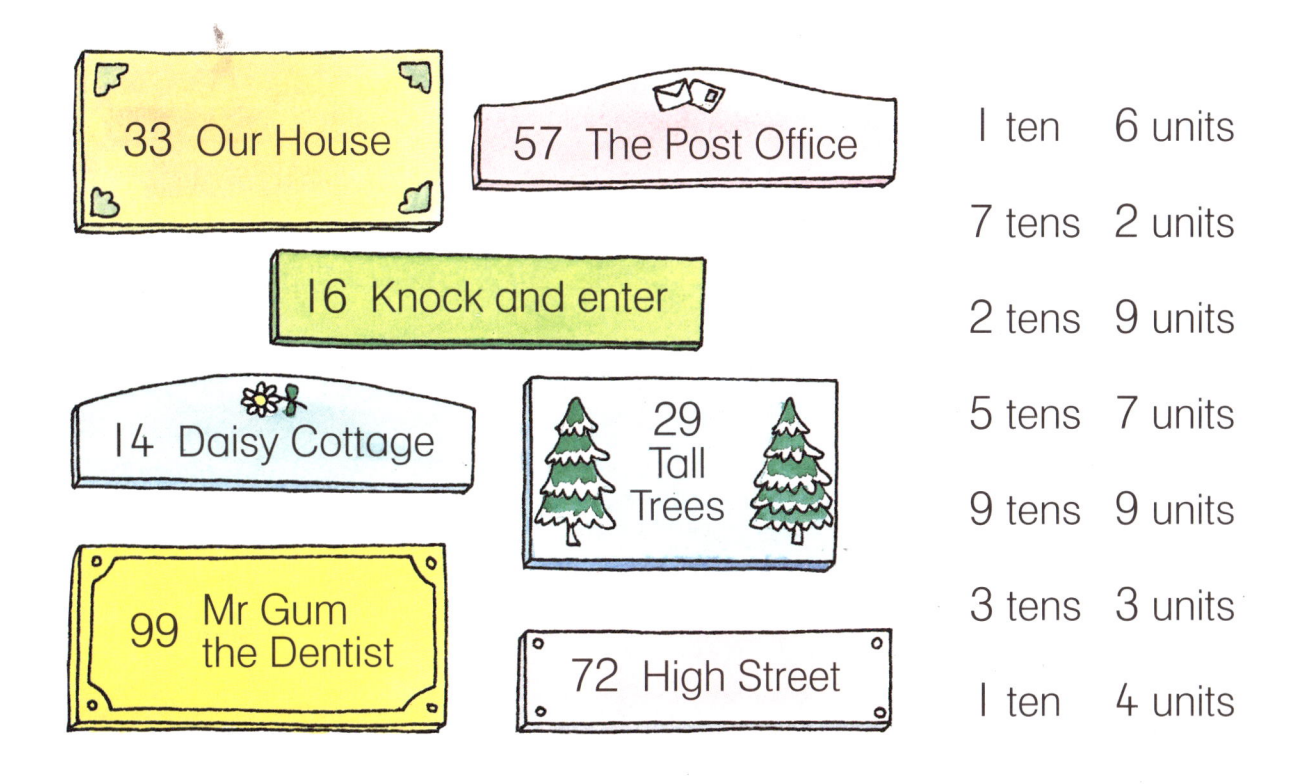

33 Our House

57 The Post Office

16 Knock and enter

14 Daisy Cottage

29 Tall Trees

99 Mr Gum the Dentist

72 High Street

1 ten   6 units

7 tens 2 units

2 tens 9 units

5 tens 7 units

9 tens 9 units

3 tens 3 units

1 ten   4 units

Parent point: Help your child understand place value by playing grouping games with coloured buttons or pasta shapes. Practise breaking down numbers into tens and units; show where the tens must go and where the units must go when writing numbers.

19 nineteen

Addition and subtraction to 20

The Sheriff has been collecting silver coins.
Write how many silver coins are in the Sheriff's bags.

10 + 7 = ◯   2 + 16 = ◯   20 + 0 = ◯

Someone has been taking silver coins from the Sheriff's bags! How many coins have been left behind?

17 − 2 = ☐   13 − 4 = ☐   20 − 15 = ☐

17 − 1 = ☐   13 − 0 = ☐   20 − 7 = ☐

Put in the numbers at the ends of the play arrows.

8 —+ 10→ = 18   12 —+ 5→ =   17 —− 11→ =

14 —+ 2→ =   16 —− 6→ =   20 —− 15→ =

Do these additions and subtractions. Draw a line to show where each play arrow hits the target.

10 —+ 5→ =   16 —− 6→ =

13 —+ 7→ =   20 —− 5→ =

10 —+ 10→ =

20 twenty

Forest maze

The Sheriff wants to go through the Forest maze. Can you help him?

Start at the 19 – 18 at the top as this gives the answer 1. Step onto a square which gives the answer 2. Then step onto one which gives the answer 3… then 4… then 5 and so on up to 20. Where do you come out? Remember that you can move up, down, left or right but *not* diagonally.

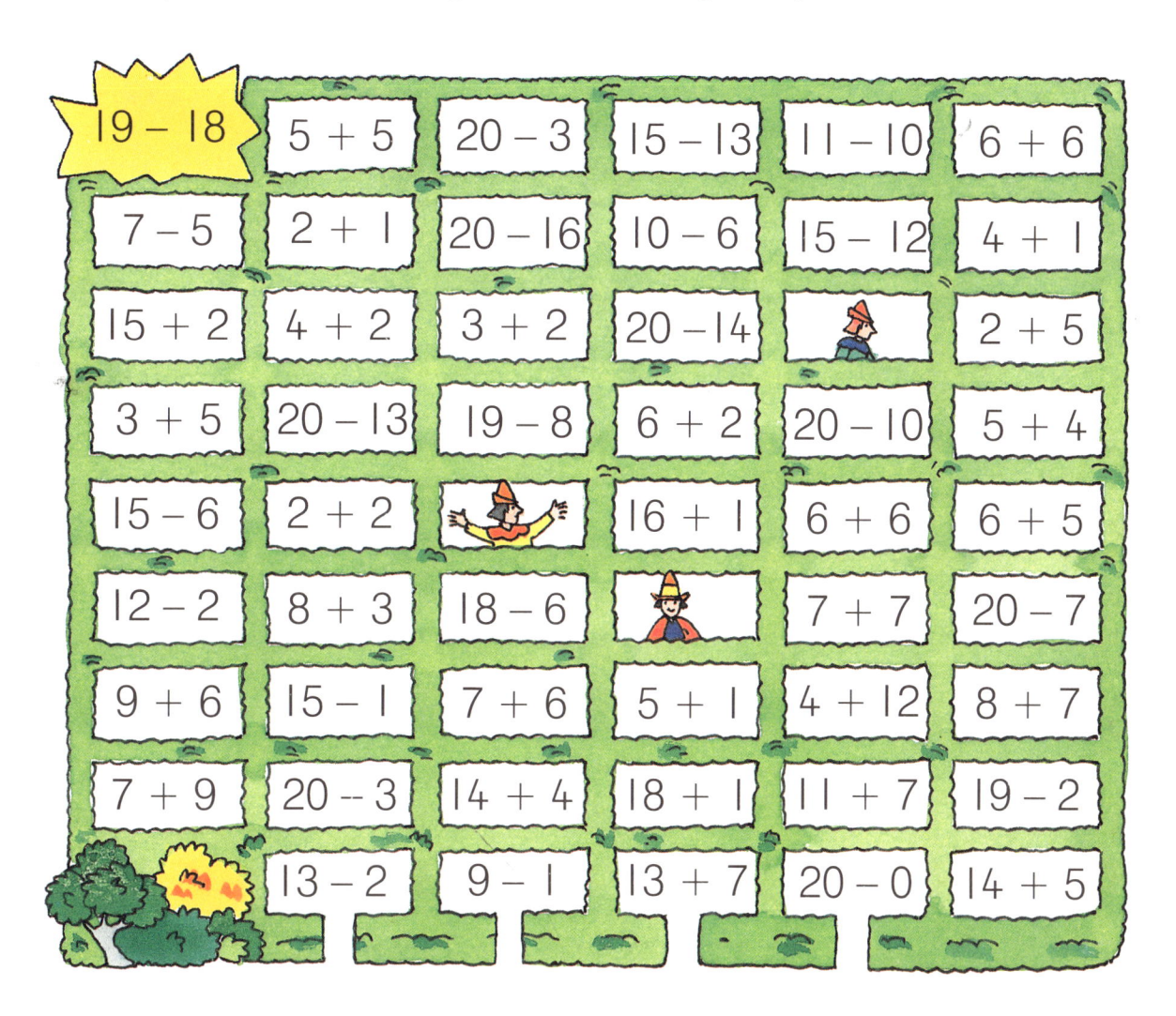

19 – 18	5 + 5	20 – 3	15 – 13	11 – 10	6 + 6
7 – 5	2 + 1	20 – 16	10 – 6	15 – 12	4 + 1
15 + 2	4 + 2	3 + 2	20 – 14		2 + 5
3 + 5	20 – 13	19 – 8	6 + 2	20 – 10	5 + 4
15 – 6	2 + 2		16 + 1	6 + 6	6 + 5
12 – 2	8 + 3	18 – 6		7 + 7	20 – 7
9 + 6	15 – 1	7 + 6	5 + 1	4 + 12	8 + 7
7 + 9	20 – 3	14 + 4	18 + 1	11 + 7	19 – 2
	13 – 2	9 – 1	13 + 7	20 – 0	14 + 5

Parent point: If children can remember some of the pairs of numbers that go to make numbers up to 20, they can do calculations in their heads quickly, and can check their own work in school.
Note also that zero has been added to the calculations at this stage.
Help your child to find other routes through the maze. For example an odd number trail starts with 11 – 10 and an even number trail starts at 15 – 13.

Puzzles using addition and subtraction

FLO   DAN

Swaps

How many stickers fit in Flo's album?

How many more stickers does Flo need for a full set?

If Flo gives away 3 of her stickers, how many will she have left?

If Flo buys 2 packets of 4 stickers, how many does she buy altogether?

Dan has all these stickers. How many are there, including swaps?

Dan gives Flo his swaps. How many stickers will Flo have altogether?

How many stickers does Dan still need to fill his book?

If Dan loses 8 of his stickers, how many are left?

22 twenty two

Let's go to the paper shop with Flo and Dan.

Flo buys 2 lollies. They cost 5p each. How much does she spend? ☐ p

Dan bought a lolly and a quiz book. How much would these cost altogether? ☐ p

How much must Flo pay for a pack of wild animal stickers and a quiz book? ☐ p

Dan buys a pack of dinosaur stickers and his Mum's *Daily*. How much does he spend altogether? ☐ p

What will Dad's *This Week* and a comic cost altogether? ☐ p

How much will Dan pay for a puzzle set and a pack of wild animal stickers? ☐ p

How much would you like to spend in the shop?

Parent point: Make a play shop with papers, magazines, cards, stickers and pencils. Use it to show how important mental arithmetic is in everyday life.

Multiplication – repeated additions

When we add a number again and again it is the same as **multiplying**.
In maths talk, 2 + 2 + 2 + 2 is the same as saying 4 **lots of** 2, or 4 **times** 2, or 4 **multiplied** by 2.

The sign we use for multiplication is **X**.

2 lots of 2   =   4

🧦🧦 + 🧦🧦 + 🧦🧦 = 6 is the same as ☐ lots of 2 = 6

2 + 2 + 2 + 2 = 8 is the same as ☐ lots of 2 = 8

2 + 2 + 2 + 2 + 2 = 10 is the same as ☐ lots of 2 = 10

2 + 2 + 2 + 2 + 2 + 2 = 12 is the same as ☐ lots of 2 = 12

Adding in 2s like this gives the pattern of even numbers.

Now you can try these multiplications using the 2 pattern.

1 x 2 = ☐   2 x 2 = ☐   3 x 2 = ☐

4 x 2 = ☐   5 x 2 = ☐   6 x 2 = ☐

7 x 2 = ☐   8 x 2 = ☐   9 x 2 = ☐   10 x 2 = ☐

Now that you can count and multiply in 2s, try counting in 3s.
Write in the numbers as you go along.

How many paws does the cat have?
Draw in more cats and count the paws in 4s.

Use your fingers to help you count in 5s.
Write in the missing numbers.

| 5 | | | 20 |

Can you count to 100 in 5s? See how far you can get.

Join the dots to make a picture. Follow the counting pattern for 10.

Parent point: Repeated addition, number patterns and counting aloud may appeal to your child more than writing out multiplications using the sign. Once your child is confident with different counting patterns, show how these may be used to aid multiplication.

25 twenty five

Division

Division is about sharing out.

6 **shared between** 3 is the same as 6 **divided by** 3.
We use ÷ as the sign for **shared between** or **divided by**.

Lin has 3 cakes to share with Rik and Sue. They have 1 cake each.

Lin 1   Rik 1   Sue 1

3 cakes shared between 3 children means there is 1 cake each.

If Rik had 6 sandwiches to share, how many could they have each?

If Sue had 9 sweets to share, how many could they have each?

Mum is having a party for Rik and his friends.
She is trying to work out how to share the food equally.
Can you help her?

If Mum had 10 biscuits, how many children could have 5 each?

If Mum had 15 burgers, how many children could have 3 each?

If Mum had 14 glasses of lemonade, how many children could have 2 each?

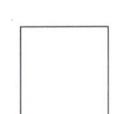

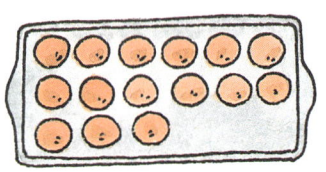

What a lot of food!

Here are some more 'shared betweens'. Try them.

4 shared between 2 is ☐ each.

8 shared between 4 is ☐ each.

Five parrots have some seeds to share.

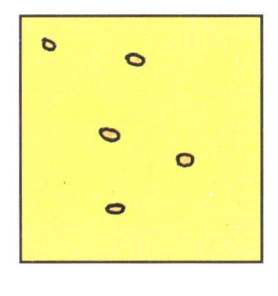

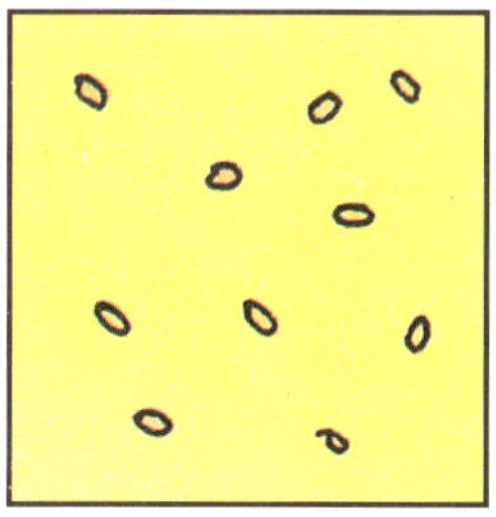

5 seeds shared between 5 parrots is ☐ each?

10 seeds shared between 5 parrots is ☐ each?

Can you puzzle these out?

6 ÷ 3 = ☐   10 ÷ 5 = ☐   9 ÷ 3 = ☐

2 ÷ 2 = ☐   8 ÷ 4 = ☐   10 ÷ 2 = ☐

Parent point: Everyday situations allow plenty of scope for working out 'shared betweens'. Sharing out food equally helps children understand what we mean by divide. Using buttons or counters can help your child with the activities on these pages. In division we can choose to look at either the size of share or how many can have a share.

Half and a quarter

When we cut something into pieces, the pieces are called **fractions**.

Whole    cut into 2 equal pieces   half   half
                                        makes 2 halves. 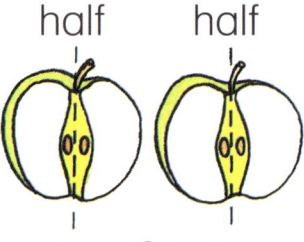

Look at the pictures.
Say which is whole and which is **half**.

Lin has 10 flowers.   She gives 5 to Sue.

Her bunch of 10 flowers has been split into **2 halves**.

Half of 10 is 5.

What is half of these numbers?

half of [6] is ☐   half of 8 is ☐

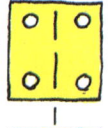

half of [8] is ☐   half of 10 is ☐

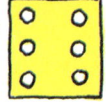

28 twenty eight

We can also cut things into 4 equal pieces.
Each of these pieces is called a **quarter**.

Whole   cut into 4 equal pieces   makes 4 quarters.

quarter quarter
quarter quarter

Look at these pictures.
Say which is whole
and which is a quarter.

Lin has 8 peaches.

She gives 2 peaches to Rik.

She gives 2 peaches to Sue.

She gives 2 peaches to Mum.

Her 8 peaches have been shared into 4 quarters.
Each person has one quarter or 2 peaches.

If 2 is a quarter of 8, what is a quarter of 12? ☐

Parent point: Fractions can be given an everyday context when you share out food.
Show that half is one of two equally sized pieces and that quarter is one of four equally sized pieces.
If you think your child is ready, introduce the symbol for a quarter and a half.
Explain that quarter is 1 divided by 4 and that half is 1 divided by 2.

Puzzle page

The challenges on this page use the topics that are in this book.
If you need help, look back over what you have done already.

Fill in the missing numbers.

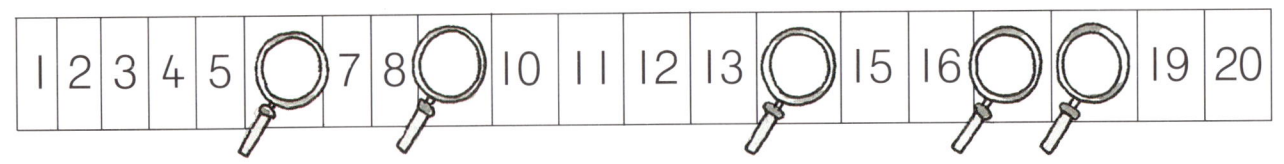

| 1 | 2 | 3 | 4 | 5 | ◯ | 7 | 8 | ◯ | 10 | 11 | 12 | 13 | ◯ | 15 | 16 | ◯ | ◯ | 19 | 20 |

Now colour the odd numbers green and the even numbers yellow.

Write the missing numbers on the robot.

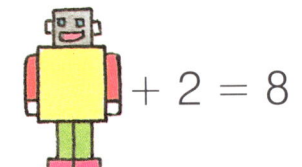

3 + 2 = ▢

6 + 4 = ▢

9 − ▢ = 7

▢ + 2 = 8

▢ + 1 = 4

▢ − 1 = 5

9 − 3 = ▢

8 − 5 = ▢

The signs are missing from these robots.
Write them in.

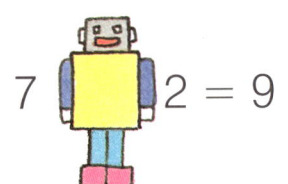

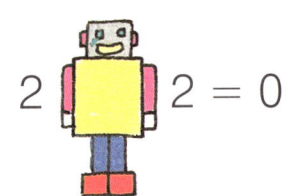

7 ▢ 2 = 9

3 ▢ 2 = 1

2 ▢ 2 = 0

2 ▢ 4 = 8

12 ▢ 4 = 3

2 ▢ 3 = 5

30 thirty

Here is a puzzle machine. When you put a number in, the machine works on it. What comes out when 4 goes in?

IN   + 2 ÷ 3   OUT

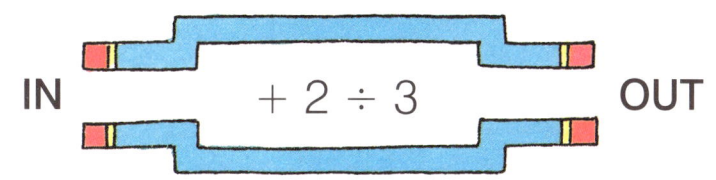

Put in 7, what comes out? Put in 10, what comes out?

Here is a whole apple.
Draw half.

Here is another apple.
Draw quarter.

The Number monster loves big numbers.
Draw the monster next to the bigger number.

91 or 19   27 or 72   28 or 82

Robot pencil sharpener costs 10p

Monster pencil costs 5p

Ghost eraser costs 8p

Which costs more? Put a ✓.

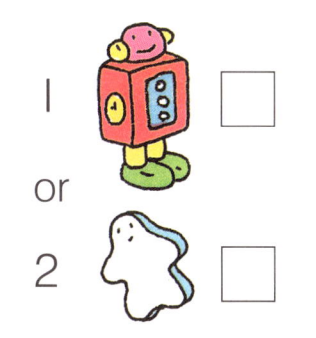

1 or 2

3 or 1

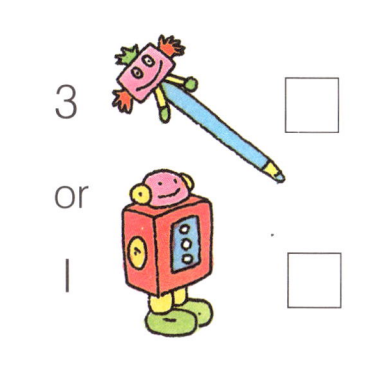

2 or 2

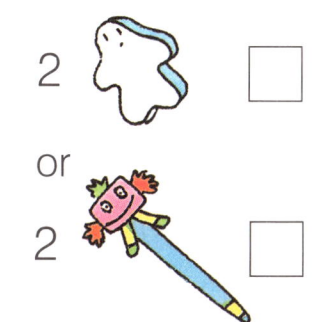

Parent point: Puzzles and number games help to make maths fun.

31 thirty one

Choose a number

Answer the questions below.
Put each answer into this puzzle machine.

Put your number **IN**   + 10 – 4 – your number   **OUT**

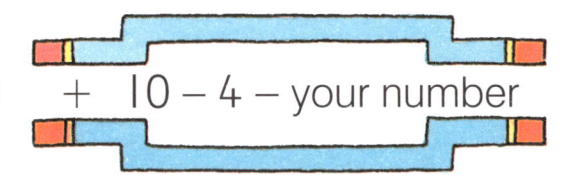

How many…

colours in a rainbow ☐

days in the week ☐

fingers on one hand ☐

dots on the dice ☐

legs on a mouse ☐

pages in this book ☐

You've done well!